DEDICATION

To my mother and father—
the grace of my night vision.

ACKNOWLEDGMENTS

Sincere thanks to my editor, Maria Maggi, who believed in this work from its beginnings and who continues to support my efforts. To Grace Roberta McBreen, S.C., whose availability and expertise have been both encouraging and helpful. To Eileen Bruyere, whose valued criticism and love of language challenged me in the past and guide me now in spirit.

FOREWORD

Between birth, which is life's first transition, and death, which is its last, there are many deaths and births. Each transition in life is best navigated in honest, deep-felt prayer.

This book of poetry is a book of prayers especially for such times of change. This is very personal prayer, very human prayer. It touches so deeply into the well of the author's heart that it taps into the underground stream where we are all one, and all in the depths of the Mystery beyond humanity which is God.

These are prayers especially for those archetypal moments of darkness when movement is blocked. Here the only vision is Night Vision. These are prayers for a time in-between, a time of neither here nor there.

Anita Constance writes poetry of brilliant clarity in its description of the experience for those who are in such a place of suspension, or for those who have ever been there. She shows us graphically what she has discovered: "the sands of the shore and the sands of the desert are the same." There is much paradox expressed here in lines of great simplicity. Each prayer has its gems, its powerful, unforgettable images.

Anger, grief, deadness, confusion, exhaustion are given voice. Yet, there is incredibly an underside of hope because it is always taken for granted that these cries have a Listener.

So many are prayers of deep, deep questioning. So many others hold answers that have a mysterious Wisdom which gives the anxious heart pause and then rest. The Listener speaks. A voice of an Other comes through not only in a different typeface but often in the surprising rightness of the answer that is made.

These poems are not to be simply read but prayed again and again. The result is bound to be movement, if not hope-filled flight.

Dr. Anne Brennan, C.S.J.
Dr. Janice Brewi, C.S.J.

INTRODUCTION

In Paul's first letter to the Corinthians, he reminds us that now, in this imperfect, only partial existence of time compared to eternity—"we see dimly." *Night Vision* is the experience, my experience of this truth.

Human life is available to many seasons of experience—from the moment of personal creation, through the moments of personal conversion. In our desire to communicate presence to one another, unlock the mysteries of life, express personal power and give all "for the honor and glory of God," suddenly, we can discover a night. Oftentimes, precipitated by crisis, loss, death in all its forms—still, so unexpected that we stumble into its depths, a death within our very selves. What was once a journey becomes a search—a quest. And we can no longer befriend old ways or draw upon energies once taken for granted.

Because this night is so different, we are frightened and confused—blinded by the night itself. Former directions, goals and motivations are now in question. What we thought important is no longer so. What we felt with conviction and abandon, we stare at with empty eyes and numb disbelief.

The past is far behind us and the future as blinding as the present. We struggle to escape this experience until we realize that the struggle entangles rather than frees us. And we think to ourselves—I was almost "home," almost there. Why now?— This is the time to be still, quiet, and to wait. Faith is on the line.

Yet, we hold within us—Truth. This Truth is revealed slowly, but we always have access to it and it always has access to us. If we are pilgrims on a journey, then it is this Truth that will lead us home. But home is not only "out there," apart from us; it is within us as well. We need, then, to learn the balance between reaching out and reaching in.

Night Vision is a book of reflections and prayer which lead to a new-life journey. It is not that the darkness gives way to light or the night to day. It is the realization that time brings with it a new way of seeing—a night vision—one that can focus, rather clearly, despite the heaviness of the dark. For "now we see dimly" but we do see—no longer dependent upon daylight, but on God-light.

The following pages are an invitation to travel the terrain of the night with the companionship of a journal—a journal to support you through the crisis, loss and grief that initiated you into the darkness.

Night Vision is divided into four phases or experiences of the journey. Each experience has its own introduction, which provides some considerations and reflection, as well as musical suggestions to further your meditation and prayer. As you use this journal, you will have the opportunity to reflect upon each prayer by writing your own personal response.

It is my hope that *Night Vision* will be an instrument of grace for you as you walk toward this new way of seeing—one that will enable you to walk through any darkness in your life...with God-light.

Anita M. Constance, S.C.

Night falls.
I want to catch it.
Fold it neatly and put it away
before its unfolding becomes a shroud
to entomb my spirit.

I feel tricked by a Magician
who is quicker than the eye.
Angry, frightened, I seek seeing—
a Shepherd's walk much too much for me.
Fearing the slaughter, I run into the night...
bumping, stumbling, knocking into its presence.
Not now! Why now?
Night whispers back: For now...For now.

Aching to focus what had blurred
in the running,
I gave in to the waiting and welcomed
mere whispers.

And then, unseeing yet perceiving,
that cloak of darkness—once feared
my burial robe—unfurled its light.
Unwrapping my blindness,
it shared the secrets of the night.

It was now about noon, and darkness came over the whole land until three in the afternoon, while the sun's light failed; and the curtain of the temple was torn in two. Then Jesus, crying with a loud voice, said, "Father, into your hands I commend my spirit." Having said this, he breathed his last.

(Luke 23:44–46)

Night can fall rather heavily, often taking us by surprise and leaving us quite shaken. It is a death experience in many ways, and so contains the qualities of grief, numbness and shock that everyone knows in the face of such a loss. It is the "dry bones" feeling that the prophet Ezekiel spoke of, when life seems shattered and hope fades. We long for God to knit muscle and flesh onto our bones and bring us back to life.

We seek God to help us understand what is happening. But even God can come into question, at very least into our questions. The usual ways of praying are no longer a comfort, and we feel abandoned—now by God.

We become acutely aware of our brokenness and emptiness. Loss leaves us poor; our resources are depleted. Inadequate, we fear to begin this new journey of the night. Any initial steps we take are tentative. Nothing is clear or sure. Confusion intrudes between ourselves and the steps we take to find a way out.

As believers, we look to God because we want to believe again…believe that God is aware of our experience, that we are loved by our Creator. We look to Jesus and come to understand his dark night, his pain, his death. It is then that we must run to him with our fears, confusion and grief. First, though, we must get to know the territory, so to speak—walk the terrain of the night; take some deep breaths and become accustomed to the reality that has come upon us; accept the death, in all its forms; admit that we are bound, held fast in the moment; acknowledge that the future is unclear and may be for some time.

Yet in all this, we must keep aware, even if the voice is small and quiet within, that this experience of the night is also an invitation to find new ways of relating to ourselves, to others and to God. We may grope around in this darkness for a while as we allow the shock and disbelief to pass through us, but this experience of night remains an invitation nonetheless.

Music for Meditation and Prayer:

"Holy Darkness"—from: *Lover of Us All*
(Dan Schutte)
"Music of the Night"—from: *Phantom of the Opera*
(Andrew Lloyd Webber)
"Be Thou My Vision"—from: *A Capella Praise*
"Into Your Hands"—from: *Been So Busy*
(Grayson Warren Brown)
"Holy Ground"—from: *Be Exalted*
(John Michael Talbot)

Am I truly lost or am I in a place simply unfamiliar? Is it a place that has awaited my discovery for many years? Perhaps I, myself, am this place... and my fears of loss merely depths of adventure and further findings of me...

I'm lost.
Will you find me?
I've tumbled into mystery
and it's dark, very dark.
Stumble...Tumble...
Darkness.
I didn't know that getting lost
would be this difficult.
Is the finding just as hard?

I hope not...I hope not!

Losing and finding...

If I could only "pull in" as it were. Keep the pieces together...apply the glue. I guess that's what God is for me right now—the glue—the Master Puzzle Player who meets me each morning ready to help me get me together...

Gather me, O healing God,
from the four corners of my being.
Draw me in
that I may collect the pieces of my life.
There, within me, gather up the fragments
and with your healing Spirit
breathe the wholeness I am seeking this day.

May I go forth, then,
one with myself and one with you—
to live each moment in holy union
with myself and with you. Amen.

Gather me...

I really hate letting go—letting go, moving on, leaving what was for what can be. I think it's the time in-between I fear the most—the time of emptiness, the not yet, the road that stretches from the known to the unknown...No matter how many times I do it, I still wish the here to there would leave no room for in-between...

The maples hold on to their leaves much longer.
They even seem to turn colors more slowly.
The transformation and the letting go
are not quite as easy, perhaps.
O God of mercy, sometimes I am like the maple.
I fight the transformation and resist my true colors.
I hold on to the branch, desperately at times,
thinking that letting go means falling into oblivion.
I resist your work within me,
perhaps because it is yours, not mine.

Help me to cling less to the fragile branch of my life.
Remind me that, at my base, I am rooted in you...
the good earth—Mother Nature...Father Creator.
And when my season comes, enable me
to greet the loosening and to float grace-fully
into the warmth of your embrace,
becoming one with you...enriching the soil—
the ground of my being—for future growth.

Letting go...

. . . .

. . . .

. . . .

. . . .

. . . .

. . . .

. . . .

. . . .

. . . .

. . . .

. . . .

. . . .

. . . .

. . . .

. . . .

. . . .

. . . .

. . . .

. . . .

. . . .

If I could only rush time, I'd find it easier to believe—at least I would believe more quickly... sooner perhaps. Why is wisdom best learned through the lessons of time? Maybe I fear that, in the end, I will not have learned...that after all the waiting I will not believe—my dreams will not come true...

Old men shall see visions.
Young men shall dream dreams.
Lord of visions and dreams,
must the young become old
before wisdom restores sight?
Could not the two walk hand in hand?
The young and the old equally brilliant,
equally wise, equally knowing?
Must time take its toll before two become one?
Which is better, to dream or to have visions?
To hope or to see? Or are both just illusions,
and what I long for...a wish impossible?

*Blessed are they who have
not seen, yet have believed.*

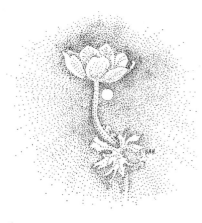

Walking by faith...

....
....
....
....
....
....
....
....
....
....
....
....
....
....
....
....
....
....
....

I was so sure of things once. I liked the music of my life. It was strong; the melody unmistakable; the beat even and clear. That seems so long ago now. Today my God of rhythm and blues plays me at will. As much as I have longed to be the instrument of God's peace, I'd settle right now to be a peace-filled instrument...

You have hollowed me out, my ever-creating God.
One day, as I stood rooted to the earth,
you broke off the fragile branch of my existence.
And now you carefully carve a new creation—
one more yours than mine.

Before, the wind had played me
and I thought the music beautiful.
How foolish to mistake for truth
the mere echo of eternal choirs.
I didn't know. I didn't know.

Now I am the instrument of your making.
No longer does the wind play the music of my life,
but does your breath instead.
I pray you then, O God, keep me hollow and free.
Keep me willing to allow you to play
whatever songs you choose.
Keep me empty of the music I may want to sing
for you compose this melody of night.

Let me surrender to your touch, it is gentle.
And your breath, it is the true Spirit of my song.

Empty yet free...

. . . .

. . . .

. . . .

. . . .

. . . .

. . . .

. . . .

. . . .

. . . .

. . . .

. . . .

. . . .

. . . .

. . . .

I've always preferred black and white to gray.
And I always thought that light was for seeing until
I looked into the sun. I'm learning that there are
two sides to everything. My perspective is changing
as I look toward Jesus...the only light that makes
the blended colors of my life less frightening...

To stand in the sun is to see shadow or light.
It all depends upon direction...
A turning point or point of turning?
Blinded by the light or blind in the darkness?

To stand in the Son is to see—
sometimes blinded by so much light.
Not seeing but seeing—knowing.
Knowing without feeling the warmth
of brightness on a sun-spread beach.
But the sands of the shore
and the sands of the desert are the same.

To stand in the Son is to see...

Light and darkness...

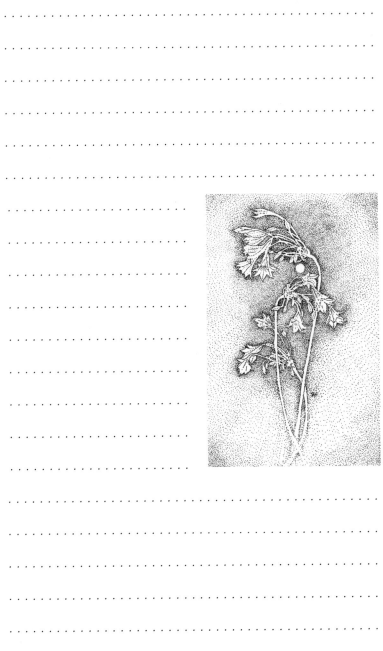

Some days, I can't help looking back. I don't know if it's necessary to fill in the gaps, or even if that's possible to do. I only hope that each tentative journey back will allow me leaps and bounds into the future...

So young and helpless—small, vulnerable, even fragile.
But in need, very much in need.
The child reached up to touch, but to touch whom,
to touch what?...No one was there
and in the emptiness, she cried.

The child grew up, still reaching up and out
    to touch.
She felt the air swirl with the turn of a skirt.
She smelled the cold air of a newspaper
coming home from work.
She brushed against soft skin and strong bone...
but she did not touch.

And as she grew so did a wall—
just high enough, just wide enough
to make reaching out and reaching in
    an inch impossible.

Lord of infancy, God of childhood,
    Lover of broken things,
extend your hands toward your little ones—
just an inch more—
and make the touching possible...

Remembering...

. . . .

. . . .

. . . .

. . . .

. . . .

. . . .

. . . .

. . . .

. . . .

. . . .

. . . .

. . . .

. . . .

. . . .

. . . .

. . . .

. . . .

. . . .

. . . .

Well, it doesn't feel like Christmas is around the corner but something is up ahead. I'd like to make a run for it but the breath gets sucked out of me when I try. It's the waiting that's the hardest—the waiting and wondering if it will be worth the waiting...

Where there's life, there's hope...or so they say.
I wonder about that as I struggle to breathe.
It feels like I am only a heartbeat away
    from something.
But I'm not sure what it is, Lord.
Somehow, I think not death because I know
you put an end to that.
But do you call this living?

Yes and no—
I do call it waiting, though...
A time in-between. A neither here nor there.
An advent of the world's making, if you will.
A puzzlement, yes,
but the pieces taking shape in your heart
will become whole.
Be at peace...
Await the birth, the arrival.
Blessed are you who believed that the promise
I made you would be fulfilled.

Waiting...

We walk by faith ... and not
by sight.

Some days, I'm exhausted by all the work ahead of me—walls seem everywhere! Maybe the problem is that, too often, I work alone...

Once upon a time, there was a wall.
Built for protection, I had said.
Built against the more powerful, I had thought.
Brick upon brick, not very high—just enough to
    separate and make safe a precious possession,
    fearing destruction.

We approached that wall, Jesus and I.
"Have no fear, I am with you," he said. "Take it
    down brick by brick, I will be true to my word."
"Much too much," I said.
So at first he did the work...
    I, too weak and frightened
to tear through safety that had settled over years.
He understood, though, and did it for me.
To my surprise, there was life and we walked away
    hand in hand.

Years later, we returned and there it was again.
Jesus looked at me and said, "Now it's your turn.
I am here but you will make the difference."
And so, with less fear and greater abandon,
    I undid the wall

of many years. After it was finished,
  we did not walk away.
We sat and looked at the other side—
now seeing birth, not death…now knowing life,
  not emptiness.

Once upon a time is long past…
  but every now and then
I return to that place to remember the building
and the tearing down…once upon a time.

Once upon a time...

. . . .

. . . .

. . . .

. . . .

. . . .

. . . .

. . . .

. . . .

. . . .

I wish I could go with the flow—it would be a lot easier—but sabbath living is difficult for me. I really wish I could get a grip on being held in the arms of God...

I cannot express you.
I cannot express me.
I cannot express you through me.

Be still, then. Accept the quiet.

So different for me than before.
Before I was on fire.
My spirit/your spirit burned within me,
exploded from my heart
and poured out words and feelings.
But now, no longer so.
What is different is so difficult...for me.

*For you—yes, because you think you saw
when you did not see.
I was beyond your words and visions
even then.
Yes, we touched, we felt, we breathed—
creating life.
But now, this is the seventh day.
Rest with me. Rest...*

The seventh day...

Sometimes I really wish I could reach back and start all over again. Change the script of my life...but that's impossible. I know it's up to me, though. I know I have choices—even the choice to choose. How can I make my pictures of the past into a valuable collection? It will take some honest thinking...

Wash away my iniquities.
Cleanse me from my sins.
Cleanse me from the sins of fathers and mothers
that have been visited
upon the children.

My child, listen to what you pray, to what you say.
They are mere visitors, these sins you speak of.
They are guests—uninvited guests.
When you were young, you were warned
about strangers but not about guests. You were taught
to welcome guests, to open the door and to smile.
Now that you are older, you realize that some guests
were really strangers, some guests were uninvited,
some guests sat at your table
but never shared in the meal of your life.

Today...you are host and hostess
in the house of your being...in the home of your heart.
You write your own invitations. You open the door
of your home.

Welcome...

. . . .
. . . .
. . . .
. . . .
. . . .
. . . .
. . . .
. . . .
. . . .
. . . .
. . . .
. . . .
. . . .
. . . .
. . . .
. . . .
. . . .
. . . .
. . . .

What's around that corner for me? I want to know yet I don't want to know. More challenges? More darkness? Can I make this journey without baggage...Will I have what it takes—what I need— when I get there?

Looking ahead, there's a turn in the road...
I've craned my neck to see around the corner,
but it's useless—the curve is too sharp.
Yet I have a sense of that point of turning.
My mind's eye beholds a field of dreams.
Not fantasies. Not movie visions.
But possibilities. Possibilities to be found
and taken home...to be made real.

It's a very different place, this point of turning.
I need to travel light...
because it's not so much what I bring
to the journey, this time,
as what the journey will bring to me.

Traveling light...

....

....

....

....

....

....

....

....

....

....

....

....

....

....

....

....

....

Now on that same day two of them were going to a village called Emmaus, about seven miles from Jerusalem, and talking with each other about all these things that had happened. While they were talking and discussing, Jesus himself came near and went with them, but their eyes were kept from recognizing him.

(Luke 24:13–16)

As the numbness begins to wear off and we move through the valley of sadness, we awaken to our reality, often with great emotion. There is a battle going on within us—anger comes to join our grief and confusion. We stand face to face, toe to toe, with our experience and demand—Not Now! We are no longer buffered from our loss by the blanket of disbelief. We attempt to control the flood of circumstances that threaten to drown us. We believe that reality's timing is off—as if a delay would bode better for our present life-experience or, somehow, we would be better prepared for the loss later on.

And when this doesn't work, when we realize we are powerless against our reality, we still do not give up. The battle continues. We try reason—we seek answers—Why Now? It is a way to draw comfort, if not control over the waters that continue to threaten our survival.

Whom better to address our questions to than God? Someone has to have the answers…why not our creator, redeemer and life-giver? We want to see how this all fits into the plan of a loving God. And so we plead with God…we even challenge God. Experiences from our past surface and add to our wondering. All sorts of emotions come into play as we feel ourselves pulled more deeply into the darkness.

All of our questions, whether they spring from anger, confusion or self-reflection, still express the underlying belief that we will receive an answer. This is more than hopeful wishing, for if questions are part of the journey, the answers we seek are the signs along the way. But these signs, these answers, may be somewhat veiled at times—somewhat unclear, partial, enigmatic even. Yet, they mark the way…surely. They entice us, beckon us forward, and encourage us to stay true to the path that has chosen us.

Music for Meditation and Prayer:

"My Soul Thirsts"—from: *Lover of Us All*
(Dan Schutte)
"Amazing Grace"—from: *Trust Your Heart*
(Judy Collins)
"This Day I Lead You Far Away"—from:
I Cling to You (Grace Markey)
"Only in God"—from: *Dwelling Place* (John Foley)
"Send Us Your Spirit"—from: *Steadfast Love*
(Dan Schutte)

I want to give my concern and anxieties to God...I want to, but things seem even more out of control when I do. Does God really have a plan? Can I trust God to write the story of my life...legibly?

You should have learned the Palmer method!
Your crooked writing leaves much to be desired.
It's rather unpredictable—
slanted, straight, backhanded.
How can I read the writing on the wall
when you persist in having your own style?
Before I know it, you'll become ambidextrous
and sleight of hand will be added to my story.

*I write straight with crooked lines, they say.
Maybe, instead of reading my writing,
you should become the ink within my pen.*

Pen and ink...

Sometimes my life is like the pieces of a puzzle flung into the air...pieces, only pieces. Will I ever come to recognize the whole picture? Maybe I will find the solution more quickly if I stop seeing myself as a problem to be solved. Maybe...

Where do you get all those pieces?
Why didn't you leave the picture alone?
Why did you chop up what was fine
in the first place
and put it into my hands to make whole?

I'd like things a little simpler...
At least with crosswords
there's a hint or clue, a few words for direction.
The puzzles you produce leave me guessing
where to begin.

My friend, you are the puzzle maker.
I put a picture on the box.
No one said you couldn't look at it
now and then.
No one said you had to finish it
in one sitting... Walk away a while
and let it be.
Come back and take a look...
a little at a time.
Invite me to sit down with you
and we'll do it together.

We'll finish in time. No rush...
We have into eternity.

Puzzle pieces...

. . . .

. . . .

. . . .

. . . .

. . . .

. . . .

. . . .

. . . .

. . . .

. . . .

. . . .

. . . .

. . . .

. . . .

. . . .

. . . .

Who am I? I used to know me so well...it was as easy as looking into a mirror. Now it seems I must replace that mirror with a window so that my eyes can penetrate a deeper, broader truth. Perhaps I must look beyond myself to find myself...

I heard the owl's cry again, this morning—
Who... Who... Who...
Who am I?
Who are you?
I Am Who Am.
Which is it? And why the question
especially at dawn, instead of at night?

Then again, perhaps morning
is the right time
...the beginning of time.
...the beginning of a new day.

Is not "who" the question of eternity?
Is not "who" the answer?

*I Am Who Am and
in me...you are!*

I am...

. . . .

. . . .

. . . .

. . . .

. . . .

. . . .

. . . .

. . . .

. . . .

. . . .

. . . .

As I leave the world of who I used to be, the questions of life and death become more urgent...Do I fear death, or feel the challenge of what real life—real living—is meant to be?

Like a thief in the night, death
—wrapped in a mantle of darkness—
stole through the shadows of my existence,
slipping into my home, sight unseen...
until it was too late.

Death entered, armed with silent disillusionment...
Breaking down the shelter of my youth,
numbing my brain to reality.
Time stood in motionless motion,
confounding my senses with senselessness.

How dare it break into the afternoon
of my illusions with such crashing, blinding,
bludgeoning news!
Who gave death the right to lift life from my eyes
and fling it into mortality?
To tear out my heart and leave an echoing hollow?
To close the curtain between earth and infinity?
To announce the final act, the never-again,
one-time-only performance?
Who gave death that right!?

...I did.

Moving on...

I feel like I am forever "gathering." Is it because there's a hole in my basket or that I never noticed all the pieces until now? Doesn't matter in a way...I just know that, if I stop, I will never find my way home...

A piece here, a piece there...
Once in a while, but not all at once...
I want it now—I want it all now!
I prefer a flood instead
of an oasis or two in this desert.
I have so little patience
for the waiting.
Perhaps I'll lose what I have,
if I wait for you to drop the crumbs.
I don't like your Hansel and Gretel
way of doing things!

*I suppose you don't
but the fun is in the gathering...
Just when you think
you've found the last piece,
there's another and still another.
I'm not the God of fairy tales
or a genie who grants three wishes,
but there is rhyme to my reason—
If you keep on searching,
those crumbs may just find you.*

Gathering...

. . . .

. . . .

. . . .

. . . .

. . . .

. . . .

. . . .

. . . .

. . . .

. . . .

. . . .

. . . .

. . . .

. . . .

. . . .

. . . .

. . . .

. . . .

. . . .

If what I'm really doing is coming home to myself, will I find God there already? Or is God showing me the way? Or will God show up after I've arrived? Why does it feel like God's entrance into my life is always through a back door?

Why do you do it?
Why do you come to my home
through the back door?
Why choose the servant's entrance
and come by way of the kitchen?
What are you cooking up for me?
It's just not what I expect...
You make a casual approach—
a table with a couple of chairs,
the warmth of a stove,
the hum of a refrigerator.

Yes. I prefer gathering places a little less formal,
where people can be themselves over a morning cup of coffee.
A place where we can chat—sometimes seriously,
or have a good laugh with memories
cupped 'round the warmth of tea.

Should I hang a new back door, then,
a proper threshold for you to cross?
Do the kitchen over?
Bring out the china and get rid of those mugs?

No, just sit in the kitchen and wait...
with a kettle on the stove.

God of surprises...

. . . .

. . . .

. . . .

. . . .

. . . .

. . . .

. . . .

. . . .

. . . .

. . . .

. . . .

. . . .

. . . .

. . . .

. . . .

I've been used to figuring things out on my own.
I'm trying to change that but...How many times do
I have to ask God for help before I'm finally heard?
Maybe I'm better off on my own?

"Ask and you shall receive," you said.
I used to do that, my God, but so many came
into my life before now
who did not listen...and did not give.

Is that really so,
or did you stop asking for so long
that now you fear receiving?

This is only the beginning...
I have so much to give you.
Ask...Take...Receive
with open hands and joyful heart.
All that I have is yours—
good measure, pressed down, running over.
Trust me and you shall live.
Trust me...I shall give...I shall always give.

Asking...

I don't have to look out the window to know how cold it is. I know what winter feels like...nothing separates me from the cold...nothing protects me now. Will I ever be warm again?

It is winter—
winter outside my window and inside my heart.
It is cold, so very cold.
I just can't seem to warm up right now.
I wish it was as easy as paying
the bills, each month...
I'm not afraid of paying the price.
But no matter what I do,
I feel frozen in this moment.

Then wrap yourself in the blanket of my love.
I have others wrapped there, too.
Come join us.
Wait, I'll even open it up for you—
there's plenty of room in here.
It's a way of getting through the winter.
And when this season's over,
you and my other friends can step out
and wrap yourselves in hugs—
weaving me another blanket.

Winter wondering...

There are some things I would like to forget...some things I wish I could do over, but I can't. How can I leave the past behind? I'm tied up in the "now"—bound by the past, closed to the future...Will this ever change? Will I?

A blessing or a curse,
this time of remembering and reliving?
Pain says curse.
Grace says blessing.
—The moment says: Choice.
Which will it be?
Choose seasons for wider vision
or time, restricted to now?

How does one move from time,
the now, to seasons...the rhythm of life?
How do I cradle the moment,
instead of grasping it with closed fist and fury?

It is only with open hands, only with open hands.
Hands raised, palms open,
allowing release until you are empty...until the cup
of your life has been drained of the unholy.
I take your hands in mine
and draw into myself the curse of the past.
Remember the cross? My words hung from wood?
"Father forgive them...It is finished."
It is finished for you, too.
It is finished because of open hands.

Take Lord, receive...

. . . .

. . . .

. . . .

. . . .

. . . .

. . . .

. . . .

. . . .

. . . .

. . . .

. . . .

. . . .

. . . .

. . . .

. . . .

. . . .

. . . .

. . . .

. . . .

I used to like living on the edge, taking risks, challenging the odds—when I was in charge of it all. Now my games have become a way of life—real life...

I used to like to walk along walls—
Walk a little higher than the earth.
Take the challenge of a balancing act.
Take the risk of falling.
But to be honest, the wall was never really
that high, not even very narrow.
And I knew that, even if I fell,
it wouldn't really hurt...at least not badly.

But now—I'm doing a high-wire act.
Before I was well-grounded,
but this wire I'm on is strung
from infinity to infinity...
and I see nothing below to save me.

You put me up here, didn't you, God?
I don't remember climbing any ladders
or being dropped off, but I'm here—
here, with no safety net...and I fear falling!
Where are you?
Where are you???

I am the wire.

Balancing...

. . . .

. . . .

. . . .

. . . .

. . . .

. . . .

. . . .

. . . .

. . . .

. . . .

. . . .

. . . .

. . . .

. . . .

. . . .

. . . .

. . . .

. . . .

. . . .

I was given some advice the other day. A friend told me that I am not alone in this experience... There are many others going through what I am right now, feeling all the things I feel; it's just that I don't know their names. Perhaps it would be helpful to join with them when I pray...

Healing God, touch us at our point
of anguish, this day.
That place which is known
only to you.
That place which can be touched
only by you.
No one else could find that place
and know it to be so.
Even we are unsure
of the broken places and
wounded spaces within.

Healing God, touch us at our point
of anguish, this day.
Anoint those secret scarrings
with the sacred oil of reverence
for what is yet unhealed.
—May our struggle yield
to that touch and give way
to your healing.

Amen, O Lord...

. . . .

. . . .

. . . .

. . . .

. . . .

. . . .

. . . .

. . . .

. . . .

. . . .

. . . .

. . . .

. . . .

. . . .

. . . .

. . . .

. . . .

. . . .

If I could just make it to the other side of all this. I sense the crossing over but it is to something— maybe it's a faith—greater, grander than I could ever suspect...and beyond anything I could have done to accomplish it...

The Edge of Believing.
The horizon where heaven and earth
touch...kiss ever so lightly.

The Edge of Believing.
Receiving not achieving.
Filling...with sights unseen
and sounds never tasted before.

The Edge of Believing.
Drawn into Being by being.
The Who Am
of silence, thunder and flame.

The edge of believing...

. . . .
. . . .
. . . .
. . . .
. . . .
. . . .
. . . .
. . . .
. . . .
. . . .
. . . .
. . . .
. . . .
. . . .
. . . .
. . . .
. . . .
. . . .
. . . .

We know that the whole creation has been groaning in labor pains until now; and not only the creation, but we ourselves, who have the first fruits of the Spirit, groan inwardly while we wait…For in hope we were saved. Now hope that is seen is not hope. For who hopes for what is seen? But if we hope for what we do not see, we wait for it with patience.

(Romans 8:22–25)

There comes a time when we run out of questions, when we feel emotionally and physically spent in the struggle to bring order and to make sense of our experience. We grow weary of our reasoning, realizing the need, now, for stillness and quiet. We would be happy with whispers of understanding, we tell ourselves; mere whispers would satisfy where sharp images were once our only pursuit.

The time has come for listening and for a self-reflection less rigorous and determined. As much as we may feel it is the only way we can be in and with our experience, the only thing left for us to do, it is really something that comes to us like a gift—a grace received on the journey, a grace to help us along the way.

This time of stillness is an invitation to visit our secret heart. The secret heart is our heart of hearts—the place where Truth dwells and speaks to us softly, gently. The light that we battled to find and shed sense on our experience is not out there someplace. The light is within—within our secret heart—and has been shining brightly; but because it lives as the spring lives in the seed, it was hidden. Now, nurtured by our stillness, it is discovered...uncovered. Narrow shafts of light begin to break through. They are merely wisps, at first—whispers, yet they satisfy...fully.

We begin to experience a gentle unfolding of ourselves to ourselves and to God. We begin to know God in our experience in quiet ways. It is essential, vital to the journey to reach this stillness, for our secret heart has much to tell us. It is where God waits to be revealed fully. As the prophet Elijah experienced, what could not be heard in wind, earthquake and fire will be heard in the small, whispering sounds of the secret heart.

Music for Meditation and Prayer:

"When He Comes"—from: *Have You Heard the News?*
(Grayson Warren Brown)
"That's All I Ask of You"—from: *Phantom of the
Opera* (Andrew Lloyd Webber)
"So the Love of God"—from: *Lover of Us All*
(Dan Schutte)
"Without You"—from: *Here with Us Now*
(Tom Kendzia)
"Like a Child Rests"—from: *Out of Darkness*
(Christopher Walker)

I feel like I've run into a brick wall—stunned,
unable to move even a muscle. It reminds me...

I remember the day as if it were yesterday.
The tiny sparrow flew into our picture window,
fell to the ground and lay still.
Did the surprise of not meeting open air
render it lifeless? We weren't sure...
We picked it up gently, laying it to rest
on the ledge of our home—
waiting to see if time and safety
would restore its energy and flight.
Every so often peeking out through the curtains,
we took turns anticipating its future.
It seemed a long time, our faithful vigil,
but at last the bird was gone—
life had returned and set it free.

O God,
yesterday is today and I am that sparrow now,
surprised by what seemed so transparent.
Now I, too, lie lifeless and still.
Who will place me on the ledge of home and safety?
Who will help me believe that time is all it takes
to restore my energy to fly?
Who will be the wind under my wings?

I will. I have already picked you up gently
and am holding you in the palm of my hand.
You lie there nested in safety.
I am the God of surprises but I am also
the Lord of healing touch.
If I love the sparrows of the air,
would I not love you even more?
If I raise the dead to life,
open doors for those who knock,
will I not restore you to life, energy and hope?

Time, trust, abandon to my embrace
are all that you need...I will provide.
I am the wind under your wings and
eternal life within you.
Rest...and be at peace.

Trusting the lover of sparrows...

*I know that in this journey to new life...my new,
true self, I have passed through a death. My way of
the cross has led to this death...but just as surely to
new life—With Jesus, I continue the journey...*

Jesus, I am with you...
I have climbed the wood.
With open arms and feet outstretched
I accept the nails and wear the crown.
My side is pierced.
The flow of water and blood
have washed me in spirit and in truth.
I know your thirst
and the struggle of your breath.
Sin invades my bones
and, like yours, they are not broken.

Source of life, Healer of my soul...
I embrace, with you, death itself
and sink into your spirit
as you breathe your last sigh.
For that moment, your last breath,
was the first breath of my life.

Climbing the wood...

Well, here I am—a place I would never have chosen. Is this the will of God for me? I can only hope (with a hint of belief) that God will make the difference...

Wherever I am,
I am meant to be—
for you are there, my God,
and that is enough.

The journey...

I want to be free of my fears. I want to let go of what is holding me. But the question is "How?" Only with God...

Catch me up in your arms and hold me close
until I, too, know the dwelling place of freedom.

Let me drop the fears and anxieties
that hold me fast...that I hold fast—
for I cling to things as tightly
as the bonds that hem me in.

God of freedom,
Father and Mother of the child within,
teach me to play on this earth—
to step down from your arms
and to enjoy the passing seasons of my life.
Let trust surround me, guide me,
rejoice in me. Amen.

Free me...

....

....

....

....

....

....

....

....

....

....

....

....

....

....

....

....

....

....

....

One day at a time—I can't handle any more than that. Yesterday is long past and tomorrow...well, tomorrow is too far away—just as well...

Gracious God, give me the grace of today...
the grace of the present moment,
the grace to be present to the moment.
Free me from my wanderings and wonderings.
Empty my cluttered mind, releasing the confusion
of my private tower of Babel.
Loosen my grip on life so that life may grasp me
and take me where it will.
Open my heart when I bar its door
preventing others from entering in.
Let me walk in the footsteps of ordinary time
to enjoy the dance of each day.

Let there always be a light in my eyes
to mirror your presence in my soul.
—a smile on my lips to welcome strangers
and laugh at the clowning in this greatest show
called earth.
—a spirit of forgiveness to heal the brokenness
that I share with others.
—the grace of celebration to remind me
that you are God.
—and a sense of peace, your peace,
to carry me through the rhythm of TODAY.

Just today...

God is asking me to take chances. It's not easy.
Each time I leave the home of my heart, I run the
risk of someone breaking in and leaving me in
shambles. Each time I take the risk...

I'm afraid of stepping outside, Lord.
My home is rather comfortable right now.
Why take the risk and venture outside
to find where else you may dwell?
But you keep calling me away from my security,
like a child asking me to come out and play.
Well, I did once—a long time ago—
and I came home with bumps and bruises.
I'm rather thin-skinned,
so I took a long time to heal.
Now you're at it again...You keep knocking
and I know I should answer, but all I keep
thinking about is how I'm going to look
and feel when I come home.

Maybe you could invite me in when you return.
I was once called a physician.
I helped people walk, loosened tongues
and opened eyes.
If you would allow me, I could probably
take care of you.
I still do make housecalls, you know.

Nursing old wounds...

. . . .
. . . .
. . . .
. . . .
. . . .
. . . .
. . . .
. . . .
. . . .
. . . .
. . . .
. . . .
. . . .
. . . .
. . . .
. . . .
. . . .
. . . .

*I see more clearly how much my looking back
requires me to reach out and touch the past with
peace—but it's a struggle to forgive...*

O God, I have a forgiving soul—
draw me to myself.
Let not the wall I feel between spirit and desire,
prevent me from making peace
with those who dwell within my past.

While I might not be able to forgive,
forgive for me.
You know I desire the homecoming
of heart and spirit, but at this time
I am incapable of doing the good
that I desire to do.

O God, I have a forgiving soul—
draw me to myself.

I want to forgive...

With all my wondering about the presence of God in my experience of night, I let the sounds of my fears crowd out the voice of God. I heard a "yes" within my heart, today...the "yes" of God—a "yes" that assured me that God knows my needs, fears and hopes...that God has always known...

I have wakened alone and afraid
—and God said, "Yes."
I have raged at life's injustices
—and God said, "Yes."
I have been emptied out by death
—and God said, "Yes."
I have cried tears of betrayal
—and God said, "Yes."
I have fallen on my knees in despair
—and God said, "Yes."
I have felt the sting of rejection
—and God said, "Yes."
I have struggled for my freedom
—and God said, "Yes."
I have felt the wound of imperfection
—and God said, "Yes."
I have known the pain of limitation
—and God said, "Yes."
I have stumbled in the darkness
—and God said, "Yes."

I knew my "yes," but I didn't know God's.
I didn't know, those moments
I embraced God with my faith,
God's embrace of me was complete.

And God said, "Yes."

God's "Yes"...

. . . .

. . . .

. . . .

. . . .

. . . .

. . . .

. . . .

. . . .

. . . .

. . . .

. . . .

. . . .

*Why does change seem like a nemesis to me—
always looming before me—foreboding, filling me
with fear? How can I walk toward it instead of running from it?*

O God of my strength—
Let me stand at the foot of each mountain
and throw fear into its winds,
as I watch it looming up into the clouds.
Let my lungs not grow weak as the thinning air
threatens their limits with gasping breath.
Guide my feet in sure steps
and my hands to firm grip.
May patience be a presence as I measure
each ascent, but let not lack of visibility
draw me back to surer ground.
Rather, let the clouds that rest above me
urge me up to see beyond.

Grant me courage in the middle of my climb,
when ascending or drawing back
are temptations to be reckoned with.
And when I reach the top, Lord,
plant, with me, the mark of your presence.
For without you, I would not be there at all.

Climbing mountains...

. . . .

. . . .

. . . .

. . . .

. . . .

. . . .

. . . .

. . . .

. . . .

. . . .

. . . .

. . . .

. . . .

. . . .

. . . .

. . . .

. . . .

. . . .

. . . .

As I move along on this journey, I see myself more clearly—my strengths and my weaknesses, what is easy to embrace and what is difficult...I know, now, that any change will take time. God, give me patience—with myself...

I don't have a green thumb, O God.
My lawn is filled with weeds—
dandelions, they tell me.
Get rid of them, they say.
Pull them up, mow them down.
Destroy them at the root!
But I can't. To destroy them
is to destroy me—for I am the blades of grass...
I am the dandelions that sit among them.

What then? I've tried everything but you—
I forgot you know about gardens and vines
and weeds...What should I do?

Learn to love your dandelions, my friend...
You don't need a lawn doctor.
Instead, I will give you a gift—
a new vision, a new version
of the song that is you.
Sing amen! These are lilies of the field—
make wine of your weeds...
open your eyes to the possibility
that these weeds can become seeds—

seeds for the planting of new life, my life,
within you.

Weeds and seeds...

. . . .

. . . .

. . . .

. . . .

. . . .

. . . .

. . . .

. . . .

. . . .

. . . .

. . . .

. . . .

. . . .

. . . .

*Just living requires courage—courage to get out
of bed, courage to face the day, face my fears...my
giants with nothing to protect me—or so it seems...*

There's a giant in my life, O God.
It's David and Goliath all over again.
Old covenant and New shake hands
within my heart.
David had trouble with armor and sword—
he was used to shepherd simplicity.
I'm more used to doing battle protected and armed
...I have trouble with childhood care-lessness.
Uncluttered, uncovered, weightless,
the walking is difficult for me.
I hear whispers of foolishness in my ears.
I wish I had the courage of a sling
and a few stones.

*You really do, you know.
Year by year, you stripped away
the tough-skinned mail that others clothed you in.
So now it is just sling and stones
in the hand of a youth...Daring, I know,
perhaps a bit frightening but shepherd simplicity
can be yours, today, if you walk with me
to meet your giant.*

Praying about giants...

. . . .

. . . .

. . . .

. . . .

. . . .

. . . .

. . . .

. . . .

. . . .

. . . .

. . . .

. . . .

. . . .

. . . .

. . . .

. . . .

. . . .

. . . .

Just hints of hopefulness in my life, now—I'd like a lot more. Yet, to trust even the little I have is frightening. Will these seeds make it through the darkness?

Within me, mighty God, is a kernel of hope…
a piece of the future, a spark of eternity.
You have placed it there, set it down
deep within the darkness of heart and soul
and prayed the magic words:
"Let there be life!" and life there is.
Why am I so astonished
that you actually keep your word?
Why do I question, with mathematical design,
whether your power can really be
extrapolated to infinity?
Why do I bother to question the unanswerable?
Why do I panic at the explosion of grace—
trying to control the uncontrollable,
trying to control the unconditional,
at-any-moment gift of your love for me?

*Perhaps questions are easier to bear
than answers.*

Daring to hope...

. . . .

. . . .

. . . .

. . . .

. . . .

. . . .

. . . .

. . . .

. . . .

. . . .

. . . .

. . . .

. . . .

. . . .

. . . .

. . . .

. . . .

. . . .

. . . .

I am beginning to understand that I was never lost. As far as God is concerned, I am always within sight. Dare I realize that God is never lost to me either, if I can live with mystery...the mystery of God within?

Much like the lost coin, it seems that you have
rolled away to hide in some distant corner.
Much like the pearl of great price,
you lie buried deep within some holy ground
and it is there that you say, "Find me.
Be willing to sweep your house clean and
to dig deeply into the ground of who you are."

But this game of hide and seek
isn't child's play, is it?
For what I seek will always remain hidden,
...just a bit.
I will never be able to grasp the coin
in my hand...although the search may cost
me much.
I will never be able to cradle the pearl within
after the treasure hunt...for you can never
be possessed. Instead
I must seek the corner and fall into the earth
to be where you are.
Then I will know that the coin was never lost
and the treasure was quite near.

Discovering the treasure...

It was a long road to Calvary. My cross isn't made of wood but I know that Jesus walks with me in the cross-ing...

Crossing over seems just like that, Lord...
cross-ing over.
Not bearing it upon my shoulders—
walking along, bent under its weight,
because then I'd know the journey—
I'd know the road and destination.

I can no longer "model" the cross,
reading directions and applying the glue.
It has been fashioned for me...within me.
And it is only there, within me, that I will
hear your word, and night will turn to day.

So be with me, Lord, in this crossing over.
While I may not know my journey's end,
grant me a peace-filled crossing.

My transitus prayer...

Mystery...I can't get away from it. Maybe the key is to walk into it, instead—get to know the territory and become comfortable, at least accepting...

And so it is, my God...mystery!
Let me rest in this thing called mystery.
Let me see it less as a threat and more
as an invitation...an invitation to
adventure and freedom...
an invitation to love—for you are
the mystery, you are its heart and soul.
Now, to stand at its threshold,
to look into the depths of its eyes,
is to be present to you.
Why fear falling, then?
To stumble in the darkness has the possibility
of being caught in your embrace.

Give me the grace to fly with the mystery...
to dance to its rhythm, or at times
to sit...just sit in its presence.
For, in you, darkness and light are the same.

Welcoming mystery...

. . . .

. . . .

. . . .

. . . .

. . . .

. . . .

. . . .

. . . .

. . . .

. . . .

. . . .

. . . .

. . . .

. . . .

. . . .

. . . .

. . . .

. . . .

. . . .

I remember you in my prayers, and ask the
God of our Lord Jesus Christ...to give you
the Spirit, who will make you wise and reveal
God to you, so that you will know him. *I* ask
that your minds may be opened to see his light,
so that you will know what is the hope to which
he has called you, how rich are the wonderful
blessings he has promised his people and how
very great is his power at work in us who believe.

(Ephesians 1:17–19;
Good News for Modern Man*)*

Unseeing
Yet
Perceiving

Strengthened by a whispering grace, quieted by a hopeful peace, we enter the world of night vision. Still unseeing, we pierce through the night of unknowing with eyes that no longer require the light of day, the clarity of a black-and-white understanding. Yet this perception has a tone and texture of its own, a knowing far beyond anything we experienced until now. We have the courage to continue the journey, for our dependency now rests on God and the sure knowledge that we can enter life once again—no longer fearful of the twists and turns we may meet along the way.

The gift of night vision is God-light. This gift sheds meaning on our path—the meaning only faith can give. Darkness is no longer an enemy. In fact, we come to see it as holy because it is the waiting place for light. It is only in darkness that God-light can be revealed...fully. Now we realize that our questions, once feared only as the darkness of doubt—framed by our search for understanding—hold the very light that we are seeking.

All is well in the world of night vision once we realize that darkness always holds the capacity for light—that darkness can become the dwelling place of grace, of God-light. Yes, the crisis that catapulted us into darkness did not destroy us. Like Christ, with Christ, we entered new life—a new creation. God invited us into the paschal mystery of Jesus and we accepted the invitation.

We are never the same after this experience. The crisis, the darkness that drew us into ourselves in a desperate search for safety and security, has become that dwelling place of grace which sends us forth. We begin to refocus and, with this new way of seeing—night vision—companions emerge from the darkness as well. We have not been alone on the journey, nor will we ever be. We were not as singular as we thought or even feared, so we join our brothers and sisters to make our difference meaningful to our world, for now...all is well.

Music for Meditation and Prayer:

"Light of Christ"–from: *Here with Us Now*
(Tom Kendzia)
"How Can I Keep from Singing"–from:
How Can I Keep from Singing (Marty Haugen)
"Love Changes Everything"–from: *Aspects of Love*
(Andrew Lloyd Webber)
"We Are Called"–from:
How Can I Keep from Singing (Marty Haugen)
"God of Love"–from: *Lover of Us All* (Dan Schutte)

As I reach the edge of my night, I begin to walk again...still unseeing, yet willing to search, despite the questions I hold in my heart...

My way to you is a walk on newborn snow.
There is no path to follow,
no footsteps to show the way.
Winds have swept the white earth clean...
"Walk," you say, "and make the way."
"The way to where?" I ask,
"for sky-kissed snow is all I see.
If you are there, you are thread-thin
and catch the weave of heaven and earth.
I turn and you encircle me at the edges
of my life.

Yes, I do...now walk.

First steps...

I wish I could believe more readily in the promise of new life. It always appears, however long the waiting—however faint the spark. It always appears—and yet, I continue to be in awe...

New life comes crashing in on the heels of death.
Hardly a sound, barely discernible.
A spark rising from sharply cracked stones,
as in ancient days when fire was new.
Just a flicker of light—like the first rays of dawn,
yet couched in darkness on the edge of time.
Standing on the threshold
between what was and what will be.
A delicate balance...A fragile beginning...
A phoenix rising from the ashes...
burning to the touch. There to reverence...
There to reverence...

Sparks of life...

Mary, the mother of Jesus, lived with mystery in her life...but with faith in her heart. She was awaiting a birth, too...the birth of a new life...

Blessed are we...who are present
to the fullness of time.
Blessed are we...who kneel in prayer
and raise hearts and hands to God.
Blessed are we...who make space and place
for the holy within.
Blessed are we...who are free
to allow visions and dreams to be.
Blessed are we...who welcome angels
and trust in strangers.
Blessed are we...who admit in humility
the truth of our poverty.
Blessed are we...who are open to possibilities
and smile at the impossible.
Blessed are we...who extend hands of communion
healing threats of separation.
Blessed are we...who have the strength
to be weak.
Blessed are we...who live in waiting
and surrender to the timeless.

Blessed are we...who believe.

Blessings...

. . . .

. . . .

. . . .

. . . .

. . . .

. . . .

. . . .

. . . .

. . . .

. . . .

. . . .

. . . .

. . . .

. . . .

. . . .

. . . .

. . . .

. . . .

. . . .

*I am born of God...daughter of the Trinity—cre-
ated, redeemed and healed. From the beginning of
time, this God said, "Yes" to me...*

Before I was, you knew me, O God.
You gazed on me with love
and rocked me in arms of hope.
Your wisdom saw beyond my present.
Your faith in me beheld the beauty.
You saw my greater truth and brought
into being creation, as you knew it.
What happened mattered not to you,
as much as your belief in me...
Image and likeness would endure
the test of brokenness and time.
Believing does such things.
So today and every day,
I make my act of faith in you—
for long ago, with whispered breath,
you credoed me to life.

In thanksgiving...

. . . .

. . . .

. . . .

. . . .

. . . .

. . . .

. . . .

. . . .

. . . .

. . . .

. . . .

. . . .

. . . .

. . . .

. . . .

. . . .

. . . .

. . . .

. . . .

I am the inheritance of many...Family stories touched and formed my life. But the presence and gift of generations moves about and around me still. I walk on holy ground...

The ground is peopled with life.
It truly is the "good" earth,
enriched by the presence of love and goodness...
the real food that is heart and soul of the harvest.
We are fed with these people.
Nourished by their creativity—
reaching up to us through the roots of trees,
plants, all the fruits of the earth.
They do not invade our bones with their presence.
They allow themselves to be assumed
and consumed...they are the good earth.

And we...we draw close to them
when we touch a tree, eat its fruit,
or catch the scent of a honeysuckle.
We draw close to them
when we walk barefoot in the grass,
lie in the sun, work the soil.
And we draw close to them when,
in the end, we lie down beside them...
and join in the blessings of the good earth.

(Unless a grain of wheat falls into the earth and dies, it remains just a single grain; but if it dies, it bears much fruit.—Jn 12:24)

I draw close and remember...

. . . .

. . . .

. . . .

. . . .

. . . .

. . . .

. . . .

. . . .

. . . .

. . . .

. . . .

. . . .

. . . .

. . . .

I have often prayed the creed of my faith, but now I wonder what God might say in response to my belief. In a way, I think that God believes, too...

I believe in you—
the reflection of my glory, co-creator of the kingdom
and child of my love, my blessed one:
conceived by grace—my word made flesh...
who suffers because of the poverty
within your human beauty, and the frailty
of a world that stands on tiptoe anticipation—
groaning and longing for the birth of new life.

I believe in you—
who are called to share the death and darkness
of the grain of wheat...who at times experiences
the depths, only to know the height,
the breath and life of resurrection—
at home with me, sharing the joy of my Son
who heals and brings peace in his loving embrace.

You have lived in the presence
of the breath of life whose hushed whispers
you have welcomed into the corners of your heart.
You dwell with sisters and brothers beyond
the boundaries of your home. Many have prayed
for you—far beyond your imagination—
enabling you to know forgiveness and to offer mercy.
Now, go and live because...
I believe in you!

And so I pray...

It happened so clearly that day. I saw myself as an infant and Mary as mother—mother of my re-birth, my new birth. I know I have experienced yet another level of healing...

I remember the day you gave me birth.
We were alone...No strangers intruding
upon the moment.
No glaring lights or antiseptic rooms.
No need for white coats with helping hands,
for there was no effort—
you yearned that I'd be born.
And I, I longed for your embrace.
I'd rested years within you...
the nurturing took longer than usual.
But when it was time, you knew—
and with shocking joy delivered me
from the quiet dwelling of your womb...
brought me forth with firm and loving hands
and held me high above you, wanting me
to touch heaven and come to know
my Father in the stars.
I can still see your smile as I reached down
to touch your face, for you saw it in my eyes,
you saw it in my eyes...
You saw them say, "Mother."

New birth...

I have come to know a parent-God, now—the God of Jesus. The God who comes to me more quickly than I run to prayer...who knows my nights and needs before I even know them. So my parent-God, as I pray to you, what is it that you say to me...

My child, who are on earth...
glorious are you and blessed be the name
I gave you from birth.
Bring the kingdom about, my child.
Keep me sacred in your heart
as I am in all my creation.

Today, you will have all that you need.
Forgive those who have hurt you
for my son said, "Blessed are the merciful..."

I will lead you on the right road though you
may know me not—you have my word:
Death is no more; its house lies shattered!
Come, then, sit down and break bread
at our table, and you will be filled
with the power of the Holy Spirit.
All that we have is yours—forever
and forever and forever.
You have my love, my promise...
I have carved you on the palm of my hand.

Father...Mother...Brother...Holy God...

If where I walk, this earth God created, is holy ground—why not my very self...created by God, the dwelling place of God, the dwelling place of Jesus Christ...

Holy Ground...
You are holy ground.
Take off your shoes
and approach the burning.
Better yet, keep them on
and walk, skip, dance.
There is no better place than here.
Why look any further than here?
God has made a dwelling...
God continues the fire,
within you—
present to your presence,
present in your presence.

You are good earth...
Work the soil.
Plant the seeds.
Watch the growth.

Holy Ground...

Creation has become so much more alive to me now. The summer's sun is so welcoming after the cold and darkness of my inner world. I come to the shore to rest in the warmth—and find a time for remembering...

The ocean called me to take a walk in the Son.
Warm umbrella-rays sheltered me
from the coldness of days past.
It was a day for remembering...

As I climbed over rocks,
my feet touched Peter and I wondered
if I'd be called to tiptoe on water, too.
The cry of gulls drew me upward—
I felt their freedom as they soared.
I thought of eagles' wings...
touched by winds that blow
with spirit-breath.

As waves broke upon the shore
I watched them cleanse the sands—
I became part of the washing
as they cradled my heels.
I searched for seashells,
dropped like memories along the way.
They spoke to me of hollowed palms
where fragile carvings dwell.

In the end, I rested in sunset.
Leaned back and watched my footprints
sink into the sands of time,
marking off the moments of eternity.

I remember...

. . . .

. . . .

. . . .

. . . .

. . . .

. . . .

. . . .

. . . .

. . . .

. . . .

. . . .

. . . .

. . . .

. . . .

It's strange...searching for God yet finding that God was always there, within me—maybe because I filled my life with too many other things, too many others. But you didn't let me get away with that, did you, God...

A jealous God, you are.
You want that special corner
all for yourself.
No one can enter but you.
How many times I tried
to open that place to others,
but you said, "No. Not here.
Not ever here!"
Well, I've come to say that
you can have your way, now.
Somehow it seems only fitting
that you take up that space.
As for me,
I know the emptiness is finally filled.
I'm not sure what you are doing
in that corner...
But I'm glad you're there.

God in my corner...

. . . .

. . . .

. . . .

. . . .

. . . .

. . . .

. . . .

. . . .

. . . .

. . . .

. . . .

. . . .

. . . .

. . . .

. . . .

. . . .

. . . .

Forgiveness—no longer a pound of flesh. I see
Jesus on the cross, hands extended on either side.
His scale of justice weighted by two thieves...and
they say one stole heaven. Which am I...

Is forgiveness balanced on a scale
equal to a pound of flesh?
No—
forgiveness is balanced
on the cross
where right and left
are equaled out by weights
of chosen "steal."
Robbers of the heart...
both come by light or night.
One slips in to take away,
the other to restore.
One hollows out,
the other holys in.
One cuts and tears,
the other carves and heals.
No—forgiveness
is not a pound of flesh...
It is the weightless freedom
of the open heart.

Which am I...

*Mending fences, cleaning house, restoring rela-
tionships—all part of healing. I am not alone in
these efforts. Grace continues to surprise me when
I extend a reconciling hand...*

When, how, at what point does grace
sweep in and clear the cobwebs
of an ancient dwelling?
It is hard to say, for grace, hushed
and hidden, waits for fullness of time.

We entered the house of friendship-
battered-by-storm...one taken for granted
and, perhaps, even forgotten.
Old friends, we entered as strangers this time...
hesitant on renewing ties—
neither wanting to be bound,
but embraced...with respect
for the fragile beauty we held.

Cleaning house with tentative steps,
we lifted away the dusty covers
in the hope that beauty still remained.
Memories of a home once built on love
urged us to continue the unfolding.
Would we find marks, scratches, tears
incapable of mending?
We stood ready, willing to restore
its warmth and tone.

Instead, to our surprise, our God
had been there before us, making easy
the rub of smoothness to a healing glow.
Each time we returned without fear, then...
unlocking doors and opening windows
till the winds of grace swept our house clean.

Amazing grace...

. . . .

. . . .

. . . .

. . . .

. . . .

. . . .

. . . .

. . . .

. . . .

. . . .

. . . .

. . . .

Peace finally...quiet...whispers...God of my night. Can God be here, too, as mightily as the thunder and storms that have passed over me? Funny that peace can be like a stranger—it takes some getting used to...

I have come to the quiet.
Are you here?
The wind and rain shouted your presence
but they have passed...
Will I hear whispers in the stillness?
Are you here, even now???

Peace is a foreign land
for I, too, have traveled forty years
of desert and discontent.
Now you beckon me to this inner
space and place gentleness in my soul.

Perhaps, enough then, my God...
Perhaps to be graced with this peace
is enough.

The quiet...

To be born again...to know life after death, after darkness. I have been awakened by the embrace of God who holds me like no other...

That first morning of eternal life...
what was it like, Jesus?
Did you wake slowly from that deep sleep?
Did the singing of birds penetrate the stone?
Did their song, perhaps, have the strength
to roll it away from your tomb?
Did your father come at that moment
and look down on you with love in his eyes?
The kind of love only a father has,
that loved you to this earth
and could love you into eternity?

I can see him bending over you.
Reaching down...embracing you, his son,
with warmth and tenderness—
hugging you to life,
hugging you to life.
And in memory of him, you continue
the embrace—meeting us in our tombs
and rolling back the stone
that we might embrace one another...
hugging into life,
hugging into life.

Resurrection...

. . . .
. . . .
. . . .
. . . .
. . . .
. . . .
. . . .
. . . .
. . . .
. . . .
. . . .
. . . .
. . . .
. . . .
. . . .
. . . .
. . . .
. . . .
. . . .
. . . .

With night vision, I sight my world differently. I see more than me—no longer needing light, I follow the Light...

Brother Jesus—
When the wound of betrayal cuts deeply
into the human heart,
—may I anoint the tearing with your healing love.
When my brother or sister cannot travel beyond
    yesterday,
—may I lead them through the gates of fear.
When troubled waters wash over your little ones,
—may I be the anchor of faith in the depths of their
    souls.
When spirits struggle and lose their way,
—may I be the spark of inspiration that enlightens
    their minds.
When a dark cave seems the only dwelling place on
    this earth,
—may I be a candle on its innermost ledge.
When weeping overcomes your children in the
    loneliness of grief,
—may I soothe their anguished hearts with your
    embrace.

O Divine Master,
grant that I may not so much seek
comfort from others, as to comfort them...

long for a kindred spirit, as to be a companion to
  all...
cry out for love, as to cry out with love.

For it is in the gift of self, that gifts are
  exchanged.
It is in acceptance given, that peace can be received.
And it is in entering the darkness that we will become
eternal light.

Companions...

. . . .

. . . .

. . . .

. . . .

. . . .

. . . .

. . . .

. . . .

. . . .

Therefore I prayed,
and understanding was given me...
I preferred her to scepters and thrones,
and I accounted wealth as nothing
in comparison with her...
I loved her more than health and beauty,
and I chose to have her rather than light,
because her radiance never ceases.

(Wisdom 7:7–10)

Acceptance of Change...A Sacramental Rite

THE ENVIRONMENT: A sacred space where chairs are placed in a circle with a table in the center. Candle tapers are placed on each chair for participants. The lighting is subdued.

TABLE: **Flute**—wooden and fashioned by hand.
Symbolism: We are instruments of God. The music of our lives is composed and played in cooperation with God, who is the giver of life. It is for us to keep this instrument of our life free and clear, so that we can be at peace with any song and any movement of our life's song.

Candle—a white pillar candle.
Symbolism: Christ is our light...evidence of the paschal mystery, the meetingplace of promise and fulfillment. A sign of resurrection.

Water—a bowl of water, preferably clay.
Symbolism: Water represents the waters of baptism and the tears of

grieving that often accompany crisis, loss or significant change.

Clay suggests the prophet Jere-
miah's text that we be as clay in the
potter's hands, able to be fashioned
and refashioned by the potter
(God).

Oil—a small bowl of oil.
Symbolism: The anointing of baptism and confirmation. Used dur-
ing the rite as a sign of strength in
the Spirit.

Bread—a loaf of homemade bread.
Symbolism: The Body of
Christ/one another. Bread of life
blessed, broken and given for the
life of those who believe and say
"yes" to life, itself. We are
healed and nourished in its sharing, becoming one in and with
Christ.

Cocoon—a butterfly cocoon.
Symbolism: The mystery of trans-
formation/change. "I am cater-
pillar. The leaves I eat taste bitter
now. But dimly I sense a great
change coming. What I offer
you, humans, is my willingness to
dissolve and transform. I do that
without knowing what the end
result will be. So I share with
you my courage." (author
unknown)

This rite should be celebrated with at least one other person—friend, mentor, companion on the journey of change. We are never alone in our experiences. We have one another to assure us of the presence and love of our God.

If used with a group, a leader could be chosen from the group to facilitate the rituals.

INTRODUCTORY RITES:

GATHERING:
> After all are seated, the room is darkened. The table candle is lit. "The Music of the Night" (from: *Phantom of the Opera*) or other appropriate song from the first phase of *Night Vision* is then played. All listen in meditative quiet.

CALL TO WORSHIP:
> Leader: My sisters and brothers, let us join together in prayer before the composer and music of our night-journey, our loving God. We pray with empty hands and open hearts.

> Together: You have hollowed me out, my ever-creating God. One day, as I stood rooted to the earth, you broke off the fragile branch of my existence. And now, you carefully carve a new creation—one more yours than mine. Before, the wind had played me and I thought the music beautiful. How foolish to mistake for truth the mere echo of eternal choirs. I didn't know. I didn't know.

> Now I am the instrument of your making. No longer does the wind play the music of my life, but does your breath, instead. I pray you then, O God, keep me hollow and free. Keep me willing to allow you to play whatever songs you choose. Keep me empty of the music I may want to sing, for you compose this melody of night. Let me surrender

to your touch, it is gentle. And your breath,
it is the true Spirit of my song. Amen.

LITURGY OF THE WORD:

Reading I: Psalm 139:1–12

Response: **A Baptismal Rite**

Blessing of the water:

Leader: My sisters and brothers, let us praise our
father and mother God who called us to new
life through baptism. (pause)

God of all and Creator of the universe,
through the waters of our baptism, you have
raised us to new life in Jesus Christ. Bless
(†) this water. Let it remind us of your love
shown to us when we were baptized. Help
us to live and be refreshed each day on this
journey to newness and change.

All: Amen.

Ritual: Each person goes to the bowl of blessed
water, places both hands into the water and,
reaching up, allows the water to flow
through. Each one's hands are then dried
by the person who experienced the ritual
before them. (Instrumental music is played
softly in the background.)

Concluding Prayer:

All: Before I was, you knew me, O God. You
gazed on me with love and rocked me in arms

of hope. Your wisdom saw beyond my present. Your faith in me beheld the beauty.
You saw my greater truth, and brought into
being creation as you knew it. What happened mattered not to you as much as your
belief in me. Image and likeness would
endure the test of brokenness and time.
Believing does such things. So today and
every day, I make my act of faith in you;
for long ago in whispered breath, you credoed
me to life. Amen.

Reading II: Romans 5:1–5

Response: **A Confirmation Rite**

Blessing of oil:

Leader: As we bless this oil, let us pray that we may
be inwardly transformed and strengthened by
the power of the Holy Spirit.

Loving God, source of all growth and true
freedom, bless (†) this oil so that we may be
filled with the richness of your Spirit and
strengthened for our journey of hope and
faith.

All: Amen.

Ritual: After being anointed by a member of the
group, the leader anoints each one's forehead
with the sign of the cross while praying:
(†) May God who has begun this good
work in you bring it to completion.
(Instrumental music is played softly in the
background.)

Concluding Prayer:

All: O God of my strength, let me stand at the foot of each mountain and throw fear into its winds as I watch it looming up into the clouds. Let my lungs not grow weak as the thinning air threatens their limits with gasping breath. Guide my feet in sure steps and my hands to firm grip. May patience be a presence as I measure each ascent, but let not lack of visibility draw me back to surer ground. Rather, let the clouds that rest above me urge me up to see beyond.

Grant me courage in the middle of my climb, when ascending or drawing back are temptations to be reckoned with. And when I reach the top, Lord, plant with me the mark of your presence. For without you, I would not be there at all. Amen.

Reading III: Luke 24:13–22, 28–32

Response: **A Eucharist Rite**

Blessing of bread:

Leader: Blessed are you, O God, maker of heaven and earth and lover of all your people:

We give you glory for your goodness and loving care for us. Bless (†) this bread and give all who eat it strength in body, mind and heart. May we grow as the seed of this wheat and live each day in your love. Blessed are you, holy God, forever and ever.

All: Amen.

Ritual: All stand as the leader picks up the plate of bread and returns to the circle. The leader breaks off a piece and passes the plate until each one takes a piece from the loaf...then all eat the bread together. (The song "Holy Ground" or other appropriate song is played.)

Concluding Prayer:

All: Brother Jesus, your kingdom come through me—When the wound of betrayal cuts deeply into the human heart—may I anoint the tearing with your healing love. When my brother and sister cannot travel beyond yesterday—may I lead them through the gates of fear. When troubled waters wash over your little ones—may I be the anchor of faith in the depths of their souls. When spirits struggle and lose their way—may I be the spark of inspiration that enlightens their minds. When a dark cave seems the only dwelling place on this earth—may I be a candle on its innermost ledge. When weeping overcomes your children in the loneliness of grief—may I soothe their anguished hearts with your embrace.

O Divine Master, grant that I may not so much seek comfort from others, as to comfort them; long for a kindred spirit, as to be a companion to all; cry out for love, as to cry out with love.

For it is in the gift of self that gifts are exchanged. It is in acceptance given that peace can be received. And it is in entering the darkness that we will become eternal light.

Blessing for the journey:

Leader: Let us bow our heads and receive God's blessing. (pause)

God, who created, redeemed and heals us, sends us out to continue the journey of change and newness of life in the name of Jesus, and says to us:
I believe in you—the reflection of my glory, co-creator of the kingdom, and child of my love—conceived by grace, my word made flesh.
—who suffers because of the poverty within your human beauty, and the frailty of a world that stands in tiptoe anticipation, groaning and longing for the birth of new life.
I believe in you—who are called to share the death and darkness of the grain of wheat—who, at times, experiences the depths only to know the height, the breath and life of resurrection—at home with me, sharing the joy of my Son, who heals and brings peace in his loving embrace.

You have lived in the presence of the breath of life, whose hushed whispers you have welcomed into the corners of your heart. You dwell with sisters and brothers beyond the boundaries of your home. Many have prayed for you—far beyond your imagination...enabling you to know forgiveness and to offer mercy. Now, go and live because...I believe in you.

All: —and may the blessing of Almighty God...Source of all being, eternal Word and Holy Spirit be with us and bless us (†) today and all the days of our lives. Amen.

(Instrumental music: The last phase of *Night Vision* or other appropriate song is played softly in the background. Leader proceeds to Christ candle and lights taper; all do the same, then leave in silence.)

About the Author

Anita M. Constance, S.C. entered the Sisters of Charity of St. Elizabeth in 1963. She received her M.Ed. in Special Education from William Paterson College and her M.S. from the School of Religion and Religious Education of Fordham University. Within parishes and other settings, she has ministered to senior citizens, as well as in the areas of liturgy, bereavement, sacrament programs, spiritual direction and pastoral counseling. She is also a contributor to *Living Faith*, a booklet of daily meditations on the scriptures. Her previous books (both published by Paulist Press) include *Advent Thirst...Christmas Hope* (1994) and *A Time To Turn...The Paschal Experience* (1995). The original, self-published version of *Night Vision* appeared in 1993. Presently, Sister Anita is director of pastoral care at Saint Anne Villa in Convent Station, New Jersey, and serves as editor of *Living the Days of Lent* (an annual publication of Paulist Press), pages of which are contributed by the Sisters of Charity of St. Elizabeth.

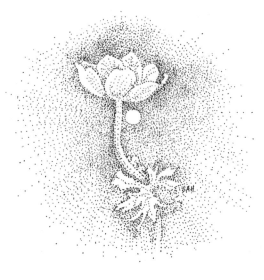